TARNISHED SILVER

JANE C. REICH

RCR ENTERPRISES

Published by RCR ENTERPRISES
Minneapolis, MN

Manufactured in the United States of America

First Printing

Library of Congress Cataloging in Publication Data
93-92612
Reich, Jane C.
Tarnished Silver

ISBN 0-9636703-0-1

Printed By: Kaye's Printing, MN
Paper: Leslie Paper, Minneapolis, MN
Typesetting: D.S. Williamson, Deephaven, MN
Binding: Midwest Editions, Minneapolis, MN
Cover Design: RCR Enterprises, Minneapolis, MN

This book was typeset with a Macintosh IIci in PageMaker 4.02 on the
LaserMaster Unity 1200XL Plain Paper Typesetter

DEDICATION

DAVID, my son who stood by my side with unending love and gave me the will to succeed.

ANN, my sister who loved me and helped me every way you could.

ELMA and HARRY, my adoptive parents who always loved me as their own and never left me alone.

JENNIFER, my birth mother who I never knew, but I understand what you sacrificed for me and everyone you loved.

JOHN, my birth father who never knew about me, but you loved my mother, your Jenny, more than yourself.

DARLA, DELPHA, JEAN, KRIS, PEGGY, VICKI, COOKIE, and BRUCE, CAROL and DAVID, JOANN and SHERM, LINDA and DAVE, SHARON and STEVE, you have all been a part of my life and are the best examples of friends, you all cared.

STEPHEN, you made me feel loved.

I DEDICATE MY SUCCESS AND LOVE TO YOU ALL.

JCR 1993

...one comes into this life alone and one leaves this life alone.

...what shapes your life is the information you are given and the exposure you have.

...if you are given truths you live by truths.

...if you are given lies you live by lies.

...until one day your inner soul seeks the truth and finally sets you free...

How many times does a life take a turn from the time of birth until death? Some changes are made by ourselves and some by others in our lives and some are made from the circumstance of life. Why do they happen and what determines the time of each change?

Life does not change as the seasons do when the last green tree of summer turns a brilliant gold or red in a matter of a week or two and then suddenly all the leaves have fallen and the trees are bare and the winter snow covers the land like a blanket protecting life from the harshness of the season to come; timed perfectly, the warm rays of the sun wake up nature in the spring, suddenly the earth bursts forth, renewed and ready for a new beginning.

Changes in one's life happen suddenly and not timed as in nature. They can happen as violently as nature's storms or as peacefully as delicate falling snow. They can happen in the best of times or the worst, but they always change our life.

Two years ago J.C. said a final good-bye to the man she loved desperately. That night was etched in her heart forever. How far she had come since that painful night. Only J.C. and her son Michael knew, as he was by her side through all the pain and heartache. It was the way it had been since Michael was born seventeen years before. He was truly her flesh and the only person she really trusted in her life. He loved her and never lied to her unlike almost everyone else who professed to love her. She knew what real love was and J.C. also knew what lies were and she had unscrambled them all.

Sitting quietly at her desk in the small apartment she and Michael shared, she shut her big, blue eyes and thought back to that night she had said "good-bye" to Stephen. She had lost track of him soon after that night, and of course that was for the best, but she would never forget him and he would always be a part of her heart and life. J.C. slowly smiled as she remembered that last night. It was

totally because of Stephen she had finally found out the truth, uncovered the secrets of her past, and changed her life forever. He had made her think, he had made her feel again, even if it was painful. She had her life back the one she had never really known because of Stephen.

Thinking back she could easily recapture the feelings they had that night and a warmth swept over her body. That last night, with darkness slowly spreading across the cloudy Princeton sky, J.C. and Stephen walked into the cold November air. It was the only time they were seen together in public since their reunion months before.

The staff of the Scanticon Hotel knew them well as J.C. had been a guest many times alone and several times with her son. They always took a suite on the top floor and the only visitor to see them was a tall, handsome man who would arrive quietly and leave the same way. All their meals were served in her suite, not to be disturbed.

That November night over two years ago was so different, J.C. thought. That night J.C. walked out of the hotel with the handsome man she called Stephen. He was very tall and towered over her.

The bellman had picked up her luggage earlier in the evening and was carefully loading it into the waiting limousine as the couple walked into the night air. She always took the limousine as she and Stephen would not be seen together. Like every other time she would drive quietly to Philadelphia International thinking happily of the next time they would be together.

That night J.C. had a lump in her throat. She hated saying goodbye. Tonight was not the first time she had to say goodbye, but usually it was in her suite and they would part. J.C. would go to the balcony and watch Stephen drive away and like a teenager, he would flash his lights and be gone. She would dream of him all night and he would wake her with a phone call in the morning.

That unusual night, J.C. was in public with Stephen for the first time in twenty-seven years. Their feelings for each other had always been a secret even twenty-seven years ago and they would continue to be forever. There was a connection, a spark, they had chemistry between them, anything you could say was true. They thought the same, they talked to each other freely about their feelings and they wanted everything all couples want, to love each other and be together. Stephen had even said he would move to Minneapolis to be with J.C. and Michael even though he hated the cold weather after living so many years in the northeast. He was so much more than any man she had ever known, but life together could never be for J.C. and Stephen.

Looking up into his eyes, his blue, blue eyes J.C. remembered whispering, "I love you Stephen", "I love you too J.C., and if your flight is cancelled, you call me and come back to the hotel and I will take

you and Michael back to Philadelphia to catch a flight in the morning."

All day there had been a huge fuel tank fire at Philadelphia International and flights were only leaving if they had enough fuel on board when they arrived in Philadelphia to go on to their destinations. Additional fuel could not be loaded on the planes after landing as a spark from the flames could ignite and cause a disastrous explosion.

The phone lines were so jammed that the only way to see if your plane was leaving was to go to the airport and hope you got out.

Stephen quickly leaned down and took J.C. into his arms and looking into each other's eyes, their lips met. The passion, the love, and the endless longing, were all there but the time was not. Neither spoke about seeing each other again, or when their life together was to be.

This was good-bye and J.C. pulled away instinctively and turned to step into the waiting limou-

sine. She knew the feeling of loss, of hurt, of pain that you can't stop with a pill. She had felt the same pain and loss twenty-seven years before when she said good-bye in high school. The time was not right then and she didn't think she could bear the pain but she did and she would again, for she was a survivor and she had been taught to handle her true feelings. You hide your true feelings and pretend, live in a fantasy world and everything would be all right. J.C. knew that game so well. She was the expert at hiding her feelings.

As the door shut and she settled back into her seat for the trip to the airport, she was numb. She had no tears, her eyes were dry. She stared into the night sky. She had experienced a dream of being with Stephen and it was over. He wasn't free and she never expected him to be. It was too late for them, too many things had happened, she was too damaged from her past, too tarnished, she could not have a successful relationship and now she had to face the fact that the

only man she truly loved was gone for good. Their time together could never be.

J.C. had to be strong for Michael. He would want to know how Stephen was as soon as they met at the airport and she would tell him that Stephen would be with them in Minneapolis soon. That was a lie, just another lie to protect someone from hurt and rejection and pain. It was over!

That was two years ago. Opening her eyes, J.C. felt a tear run slowly down her cheek. She felt a little pain and the loss would always be there, but time softens the memory. It was over she thought. You could never recapture what they had. Together they lit up each other's lives. If I knew forty-years ago or even twenty years ago, what I know now, my life would have been so different she thought.

She had adored her Daddy and Mother but there was so much they wouldn't tell her and so much hidden in her own mind that they never knew.

J.C.'s memories had been locked away. The lies, the deceptions, the secrets her whole life. For J.C. it had almost destroyed her not knowing the truth. Her whole life had been based on lies not truths. Her parents loved her but out of fear and acceptable practice in the forties they hid the truth. Peter her husband for fifteen years had lied and even a year ago Stephen denied loving her, that he only felt sorry for her.

J.C. had learned that if you live by lies that is what your life becomes...she was given lies to live by, not truths. She was living her life now with truths, but for all her life until a year ago her choices had been based on lies. Not even J.C. could be expected to make the right decisions with everything that had happened to her.

She had lost friends seeking the truth, she had lost Stephen and even her Mother couldn't tell her before she died. J.C. understood, but the confusion as a child, the pain and the loss in the last few years were

almost too hard to bear. She retraced her entire life. J.C. knew very well how strong her parents were, how they did everything to protect her and her sister Ann.

Yes...J.C. knew all the truth even truths her parents never knew and she was grateful for that. She knew every lie as well. Most of all she knew exactly when the lies began. In Silver City the lies began. They began the night she was born!

J.C. knew what she wanted to do. Stephen had been the key to unlocking everything in her mind so she could remember, so she could survive. She could change, she did change!

She had the same heart, the same body, the same blue eyes, but she had changed. She wasn't afraid anymore, she knew herself so very well and she knew everything about her life. She wanted to tell Stephen, to thank him. He was always the person she could tell everything to even when they were so young. It was just so easy to talk to him. He always

listened and he always understood. He would never expect to hear from her again, but he was right about everything.

She hoped time was on her side, she didn't even know where he was it had been two years and his life had been as unsettled as hers. It didn't matter, she would send the letter thanking Stephen to his last address and maybe luck would be with her and the letter find him. She had to let him know that what he had told her had changed her life.

For a moment J.C. almost felt a little excited thinking about Stephen, but she knew too well, it was over for them. She knew she would not have survived if he hadn't been in her life again after so many years. He would understand, he always did.

Carefully she pulled open her desk drawer and she took out a piece of linen paper. She picked up her pen and started the letter......

writing so easily......so familiarly;

Dear Stephen,

Two years have past since I saw your face
and touched your hand or kissed your lips, but time
eases the loss. I know we parted on the worst of
terms not the best and I want you to know what
happened. I did not know why I acted the way I
did toward you or toward anyone. I had no idea at
the time what was happening to me or what drove
my life and my actions. I know now. That is why
I am writing you today. I found the truths for the
most part. I have cried a lot of tears, and I have
tried to make the most painful times more humor-
ous so they were easier to bear. You know me,
smiling on the outside and crying on the inside.
Because of you I found the truth or I unlocked the
truth in my mind that had laid hidden since I was
five years old. I tried not to remember, I fought
the past, but once the flash backs came, my life
patterns became a map of my life. Everything I

did was there and the most important part, why I did so many things I couldn't explain nor could anyone else really understand. The only thing I wasn't sure of until recently was if the same powerful man gave me life and took it away in the first five years of my life.

I know that abuse, incest, and rape can be very graphic when you think of a fifty or sixty year old man penetrating a five year old little girl. That is exactly what happened to me and maybe as many as thirty percent of the women today. It isn't pretty and it isn't nice! It is violent and shocking and horrid.

You understood how hard my life had been when we were together, but even you did not have half the truth that I now have. After we parted, there was so much more yet to be uncovered. I had only scratched the surface of my past.

Stephen, I had to thank you because other than Michael, you were the one who helped me

find my life. I know a year ago you denied loving me and that you felt sorry for me and that I was a fatal attraction, but you were so wrong. You see you loved me more than almost anyone because you told me the truth and I listened.

Oh, it took me a while to figure it all out and it wasn't easy feeling the pain or surviving financially, but I had to take the responsibility of my life, of my actions and change the choices that seemed to be deeply programmed into my mind. I had been in pain for so long that I was numb to just about everything except when it came to you. The things you said to me made me feel loved like I never had in my life, so it didn't really matter if you meant it or not. I felt like you really loved me. You awoke my feelings. You helped me reclaim the feelings I lost so many-years ago.
I'll explain!

You know so well how we grew up in Silver City. It was not much different from any other

southwestern town. The town was rich in western history. There were the silver strikes out on Chloride Flats by the Bullard Brothers, and the gold mining in Pinos Altos, the Indian Raids, Billy the Kid and the bar room brawls. Silver City had it all.

Along with the history, the climate was ideal. Not desert like West Texas, or Eastern New Mexico, but more moderate, like a haven itself up high in the mountains. It was never too hot in the summer or too cold in the winter. The air was fresh and the blue skies were marine blue and bright. At night the clear black sky sparkled with the moon and the stars; we didn't have smog and the creeks and rivers were clean and clear. Most of all the streets were safe and the town was peaceful.

Silver City had a small downtown and Western College at the time we were growing up, so there was a diversity when the students started to school in the fall each year. Everyone was in-

volved. People helped each other and life seemed picturesque for the most part.

In the forties like when we grew up there, very little changed and life seemed pretty secure and normal, but like every other small town there were always the stories only a few knew about. The under cover gossip that people whispered about, but no one would ever acknowledge.

Stephen, you remember when we were together, I had told you that I had always known that I was adopted and that was never a secret to me. You also knew all about me finding out who my birth mother was when I had my adoption records opened, and you encouraged me to find out the truth about my past.

I had all the information on who my birth mother was and a lot of the story but there was so many things about my life that I could never put together. It took the last few years to fill in all the blanks and know exactly what happened.

My mother, not the mother you knew, but my birth mother, Jenny moved to Silver City in the forties. I know that it was a few years before I was born so, I figured she arrived in about 1942 or 1943, about the time my parents adopted my sister Ann.

Jenny was from a west Texas ranching family, somewhere around Lubbock. She had moved to Silver City to get out of the dry, dusty climate of West Texas. She had allergies and asthma and so Silver City was an ideal place to go to college. She was not that far away from home and yet her health could vastly improve. In those days, so many people came to that area for just such health reasons. The hospital at Fort Bayard, ten miles east of Silver City, had numerous patients there with tuberculosis.

When Jenny moved to Silver City, she was young and alive and ready for her new adventure away from her family. She was very pretty with

blue, blue eyes and blondish brown hair. It was her life, her spark and her incredible smile that captured everyone who met her. She found Silver City friendly like everyone does and she quickly made friends and started her new college life.

It was not too long after she moved to Silver City, that she met a young man and fell deeply in love. He was handsome and they were a vital couple, everyone could see that. Eddie's family was fond of Jenny and so when they became engaged no one was surprised. The family was thrilled. Jenny was still very young and her family encouraged her to continue college and to work as a receptionist for awhile and she and Eddie could get married in a few years.

Eddie, shortly after they became engaged was drafted into the Army. War had broken out with Japan and so he had to leave his young fiance and go away to fight for his country. Like many young men from Silver City he was a prisoner of

the Japanese and was among the group that they thought were killed by the Japanese. Eddie had been gone for so many months and no one had heard from him and so everyone was beginning to believe he was dead. There were so many casualties that it was a very real possibility.

Jenny was faithful and loyal to Eddie, but even his family encouraged her to go on with her life. She was too young to give up year after year, waiting and hoping for his return. Jenny was not anxious to start dating anyone. She was very loyal and had felt she belonged to Eddie.

She started going out with groups of friends and she liked it that way. There were a couple of brothers in Silver City who were so nice to her and very friendly. She did not know a lot about them and they did not mix with a lot of her friends, but she liked them both and especially John who was so good looking and tall. He had beautiful blue eyes and dark, thick wavy hair. He had asked her

to dinner several times, but she never accepted. Lots of men asked her to dinner, even old Dr. Robert Watson, the distinguished doctor in Silver City who was known to prey on any good-looking women.

Dr. Watson had come to Silver City as an Army doctor to work at Fort Bayard Hospital and remained in Silver City after his duty was over. He and his wife, Alyse moved to Silver City from Kentucky. He had a reputation of being a fantastic surgeon. He had his home and clinic combined into one on Cooper Street, next to the Grant County Court House.

Jenny never accepted his invitations for dinner, nor would she ever consider working for him as a receptionist. She had refused all of his advances and she was well aware of the gossip about the great Dr. Robert Watson.

Dr. Watson took care of everyone. He made house calls, he delivered babies, he saved lives and

he used his power and wealth to control any way he could. Nobody ever questioned his actions or his indiscretions. Only his wife, Alyse, suffered quietly, by herself, alone. She knew the real Dr. Watson. His brilliant mind and skill could never be questioned but his private life was a well guarded secret that only a few knew.

Dr. Watson had an insatiable lust for women. He didn't care if they were married or single. He once gave a married woman a piano as a gift for her favors to him and her husband bragged about it. He could buy woman and he could do anything he wanted with them and a lot of women were afraid to refuse his advances, Jenny did and that did not please the Dr.!

He was skinny and Jenny was totally re-pulsed by him. He would fondle women in his office, he would trap them at night and anyone who got pregnant he could easily give an abortion to. Two of the women he did impregnate refused

abortions so Dr. Watson kept a son and a daughter and his devoted wife raised them as their own. It was rumored that he had other children that he adopted out in northern New Mexico. Nobody ever questioned this man. He had power. He could give you life and he could take it away.

Stephen, for years I thought I was just another mistake by Dr. Watson and that is why my parents never told me anything about my birth. They were protecting him and me from shame. Nobody crossed this man, but Jenny was strong and she refused him.

Jenny was grateful for John, she finally had someone to start dating and maybe Dr. Watson would leave her alone.

Eddie had been gone a long time and so reluctantly Jenny started dating John. They would go for long rides or they would go to dinner and walks and the movies, or they would spend endless hours just talking and being together. John was

smart and strong and soon John realized he was in love with Jenny. He knew that if he told her it would be hard on her since she had been engaged to Eddie and had been loyal to him for so long.

What John didn't know was that Jenny was falling deeply in love with him. Maybe she was just so tired of being away from her family or maybe this love was meant to be, but when John asked her to marry him she accepted readily and was thrilled! They had totally different backgrounds, but Jenny never cared much about that, she cared about how the person was inside and she knew she was in love with John.

Her family, even though they were Catholic and John was not, they would just have to accept him and love him as her husband. John was with her and they were young and in love and that was all that mattered.

John graduated from college in June and they planned to get married in the fall of 1945.

John was to go to his new job and Jenny would stay in Silver City and plan for their wedding. The Sunday before John was to leave, Jenny had made a special dinner for him at her apartment. There was wine and candlelight and John never left that night. They were two people in love, planning to get married. They were passionate about each other and they spent that last warm June night making love. John left the next day for his new job and Jenny was so happy. John was in the States so she wasn't concerned about him coming back, like her former fiance, Eddie.

August came around and Jenny realized she was pregnant. I'm sure she felt like any girl does when that happens, but in the forties it was totally unacceptable. I think that a lot of people still feel that way but mistakes happen and one certainly shouldn't be branded for life. But in a small town like Silver City you certainly would be.

Jenny was pregnant, unmarried, not a virgin, a Catholic girl. Her life could easily be ruined. People would talk and it would be hard on John too. He already had to deal with so many ignorant people who judged him as less than they because he was not of a similar background. People could be so cruel. John would still love her and they could move away and nobody would know. She could hide her pregnancy and she could not get an abortion, there were no legal abortions and that wasn't an option for Jenny anyway. She wanted John's baby desperately. She loved John more than herself, and he would be back soon so she kept silent...the secret was hers alone. She felt wonderful so everything would be fine.

In late September just before John was to be back, Jenny's life fell apart again. One morning she received word that Eddie had been found alive and was on his way home to her. He had survived the ordeal of being a prisoner of war and was free

to come home. What in the world was Jenny to do? She had changed her whole life, she was to marry John in a few weeks and she was carrying his baby, but she had loved Eddie too.

John's mother who still lived in Silver City had heard about Eddie's return and let John know right away. She knew how much John loved Jenny and she adored Jenny, but she knew with their differences in their backgrounds, it was not going to be a simple marriage. Families are all alike. Parents only want their children to marry into the same kind of background, and that would be wonderful , but love doesn't always work that way. Love happens and when it does and you are lucky you should capture it and cherish it forever and that is exactly what John and Jenny had intended to do.

Before Eddie was to return, John made a quick trip home to Silver City. He knew Jenny was torn and he loved her desperately. She had

waited and waited for Eddie and then started her life with John.

John thought that maybe life was telling him something. Maybe her family would never accept him and Jenny would have to chose between them. He could never have her do that, he loved her too much. John talked to Jenny for a long time and stayed with her again and they made love all night with Jenny crying. She didn't want to give him up, but what would she say to Eddie?

In the morning when Jenny awoke John was gone. He had left her a long letter saying she belonged to Eddie and that they would have more of a chance at a successful marriage than she and John would have. He told her that he would always love her and would never forget her special smile, her blue, blue, eyes and her thick hair and especially how kind she was to everyone.

Jenny was shocked because she loved John so much and he didn't know but she had his life

deep inside of her body. She had his baby growing inside of her. Some of the sparkle left Jenny's eyes that day, the day she read John's good-bye to her. She lost part of herself, and she never was the same again.

Before she could even think, Eddie was home to a war hero's welcome. Eddie dismissed the facts that his family told him that she had almost married John, he didn't care. John was gone and he was there and he was going to marry Jenny no matter what his family thought. They never approved of John. They did think Jenny should find somebody else when Eddie was missing, but not John.

In November of 1945 Jenny and Eddie were married in Albuquerque. His family was not there but Jenny was determined to make it work. She was pregnant and she would tell Eddie soon, but not yet. He never suspected anything. She was always thin and she was so modest around him and

very quiet. Eddie just figured the adjustment to marriage and the shock of him coming home was normal after so long. He hated to tell her that he had to go back to Japan in December, but Jenny took it well. Frankly she was relieved for the first time in months. She had not even seen a doctor and she figured she was five months pregnant.

As soon as Eddie left, she went to see Dr. Watson. She couldn't stand him, but she had to have medical attention and she had to get the baby born. It was John's baby and she would do anything to give this baby, her baby, a chance. It was all she had left of John.

As soon as Dr. Watson saw her, he saw his next victim of prey. He was solicitous and overly friendly. Jenny told her story to the Doctor and he listened carefully. Of course she could not keep the baby, why would she want a baby by John for heaven's sake. This baby did not have the right parentage, but he could certainly solve all of her

problems. He understood she thought she loved John, but it was all wrong. He tried to touch her and that was easy to do as he had to examine her. How could he be so lucky. She would be disgraced if she kept the baby. She had to give this baby away. He gave her vitamins to build her body up and said he would make all the arrangements.

Jenny didn't trust him for a minute, but she had no choice. He was a good doctor, but he was so sick and he always had one thing on his mind...how to satisfy his sexual needs. He thought he was so much better than anyone else and he even sounded like Hitler the way he talked about John.

When Jenny got home that day she knew John was probably right because she had lost friends when she dated him. She saw the stares and heard all the whispers. John was a wonderful person and he was no different than anyone else

and he loved her and she loved his baby. She just wished John had known. John was a lot better person that someone like Dr. Watson who ran around on his wife.

Jenny had heard all the stories how he had drugged women for sex and how mean and cold he was to his wife. But she had to get this baby born and neither John or Eddie or anyone could know about it so she had to make the only decision she could. Give my baby up and nobody but Dr. Watson would know who the father really was.

Stephen, by this time Dr. Watson was delighted. He would be a hero again to Elma and Harry. They would love another baby and that would make them indebted to him forever.

Elma would always come and stay with Alyse if she got sick again or tried to commit suicide. Elma and her mother Mae were devoted to Alyse and they would never say anything to anyone. He could stay out all night on his rounds.

The ones he enjoyed, sleeping with his pick of the month.

Elma and Harry were devoted to the baby girl he got them three years before. She was one of the mistakes old "Cap" made with his secretary. She checked into the hospital and Elma and Harry paid all of her expenses and had a beautiful baby girl. Elma and Harry had plenty of money and could give another baby a good home.

Oh, this was so perfect for Dr. Watson. It was so easy when you are a doctor and in a small town besides. You can control everything and everyone and Dr. Watson even thought maybe he could get a little action out of Jenny. She would be so grateful to him. He had always wanted to get his hands on her, she had such gorgeous hair and terrific body. She was so scared someone would find out. She needed him to make everything work out for everyone in her life, and he could handle everything so easily.

When February 1946 arrived, Dr. Watson had all the plans made. He made arrangements for Jenny at the Bullard Hotel as she could not be in her home. If someone came by unexpectedly the plan would not work. The Bullard Hotel was home to many of his late night activities and he always kept a room there. Of course he never told Jenny it was his room that she was to stay in. Jenny agreed to all the plans although she hated herself for having to depend on the lecherous Dr. Watson. She was nine months pregnant and had no choice.

Early in the morning of February 23, 1946, Jenny awoke with pains and she knew the time was near. She could only hope that Dr. Watson would be where he said he would be. As she called the number he had given her, she was cold and tears were streaking down her cheeks. Luckily, Dr. Watson answered right away and their plan was to begin. Dr. Watson picked Jenny up and

took her to the hotel. She laid down on the bed and the Doctor examined her and told her the baby was hours away. He left, of course, and Jenny was a little scared being left alone, but she didn't want him there and she didn't want this time to be shared with anyone.

She was so alone. It was cold and the wind was blowing outside. In February the wind always blows in Silver City. Jenny hated the wind. Why was she so alone at a special time in her life, but it wasn't special. John didn't know he had a baby on the way and Eddie her husband was far off in Japan not knowing what she was going through by herself.

By late afternoon Jenny became frantic with pain and by the early evening when the doctor returned Jenny was weak and pale. Dr. Watson hadn't called all day but he was a skilled doctor and Jenny was grateful he was finally there. Slowly and surely a frail baby girl was making her

presence known. Crying softly, Jenny saw the baby. She was so tiny but she was alive and her color was good.

Quickly Dr. Watson wrapped the baby in a green army blanket and handed her to Jenny. Looking down at this little miracle of life, Jenny knew what she had to do but could she be so strong.

Softly she whispered to her tiny little girl, "I'm doing this for you and I love you very much. Be strong and grow up brave and know your Mother loves you and your father very much."

Dr. Watson took the baby from Jenny and told her he would be back. Jenny gave her baby a soft sweet kiss on her face and touched her tiny little hands knowing she would never hold her again. Sobbing, pale Jenny turned away as Dr. Watson left. She would never get over having to give her little girl away, never, as she cried herself to sleep.

Jenny awakened hours later and the bed was wet and she was burning up. She could see blood all over the bed. Where was Dr. Watson, he hadn't been back. He was probably with one of his girlfriends celebrating. With all the strength Jenny could gather she pulled the phone over and tried to reach Dr. Watson. No answer. She knew she was in trouble and she felt weak and the room was so hazy.

Scared but having no choice she dialed Eddie's sister and luckily she answered. Jenny told her she was very sick and please come and help her. Eddie's sister picked up Eddie's mother and the two of them went to the Bullard Hotel late that night. Shocked, they found Jenny weak, hungry and bleeding to death.

Dr. Watson had left her to die. Nobody knew he had even been there and he had his prize. Anyway, Jenny gave herself to that John but not to him so who cared about her. He would do what he saw

fit to do with the baby and nobody could ever tie him to the birth at all.

Eddie's sister and mother saved Jenny's life that night and Jenny carefully told them she had a miscarriage. From all the blood and condition Jenny was in, the story or lie was logical. Everyone assumed the lost baby was Eddies'.

Nobody ever knew in Silver City that a baby girl was born in the Bullard Hotel that cold February night so many years ago. Jenny knew and Dr. Watson knew and he alone took that baby for his own use that night, she was his to do as he wished and Jenny had no choice.

That little baby girl wrapped in an old, dark, green, army blanket, not even cleaned up from birth was taken to 1823 Yucca Drive that night. She was frail and tiny and he the doctor had changed her life that night forever. He picked her out of her mother's arms, and he made the choice for her, but he wasn't finished. He had delivered

her into the world, he had given her away, and he would destroy her before she had any chance of making her own choices. Yes, his best work was yet to come.

Stephen, you know who that baby girl was. That baby girl was me and it took only one man, one powerful man to bring me into the world and destroy it for me in the first five years of my life.

That first night of my life my Aunt Gladys took care of me. She cleaned me up from birth and she kept me by the oven all night to keep me warm. She and my Uncle Charles found Mother and Daddy in Globe, Arizona that night.

They had gone with friends to Phoenix to pick up a new Jeep. They were on their way back to Silver City and were spending the night in Globe. Mother told me that they were so excited to have another baby, that when Uncle Charles got in touch with them, that they didn't even ask if it was a boy or a girl. They went out and celebrated

and came on home to Silver City the next day. They were always so happy to have children after trying for so many years and losing babies in childbirth.

You know that really hateful people around Silver would taunt Mom and Dad that they knew who our real parents were and that we were mistakes. Some of the men in town went as far as to say Daddy wasn't a real man because he couldn't father his own children. Finally Daddy had enough and took them to the Masonic Cemetery and showed them the grave of my sister that died an hour after birth in September of 1942, the year before Ann was adopted.

I was not a very healthy baby and I almost died twice the first year from a blood disease and an enlarged thymus gland that cut off my oxygen. I could not digest food very well and was constantly sick to my stomach. But Mom and Dad always saw to it that I had the best of care. My

parents would rush me to El Paso to get huge doses of X-Ray to control the enlarged Thymus gland. Of course Dr. Watson was always available to Mother and kept her on his good side. He did plant fears in her, that maybe our mothers would come back for us, so she was overly protective our whole life. I'm sure they were relieved when the adoption papers were filed on both of us and the adoptions were legal. That never stopped the gossip although Ann and I never heard anything but I always felt I was different from Ann, that there was something about my past that was unspeakable. I always knew I was adopted and it did embarrass me when Mother would make a big deal of it. Kids want to be alike, not different.

I grew pretty normally until 1951 when I was five years old and that was the year my life ended. I was never really strong, but I always felt happy and I had a good personality. I was easy to be around. I spent lots of time with my Daddy as

Ann was in school all day. In June of 1951, I was rushed to Hillcrest Hospital and I had an infected appendix. Dr. Watson removed it as it ruptured filled with gangrene. I was in the hospital a few days and then I went up to Dr. Watson's clinic on Cooper Street to have the stitches removed. I wasn't afraid of him then. I never really liked him. He was always cold and would never talk to you. He would talk around you, like you the patient did not exist. I remember he had beautiful nurses that were always so kind and for some reason they were always big busted. I thought that was funny at the time.

My weight was never a problem then, but I had been very lethargic after the appendix operation so Dr. Watson suggested a BMR exam. It was a test to check my thyroid. Since I had had so many problems early in my childhood Mother never gave it a second thought.

Early one morning in July of 1951, Mother took me to the clinic on Cooper Street for the test. That was the beginning of the end. I remember we had to be there by seven in the morning and they told me I would have to be very quiet for a long time until they did the test. Mother was allowed to read to me while I waited.

When we arrived I was taken downstairs to a room next to the big furnace. There were three hospital-like rooms. I remember I wasn't in the one on the end to the right. I stayed in that room after I had my tonsils out later that year. The room I was in faced the front of the clinic and there was a window up high like a basement window, toward the ceiling. There was an enameled white table with a vinyl pad with all those little brass brads that they used in upholstery years ago. There was one white enameled chair and a machine called a basal metabolism machine. It was on a cart and had lots of dials and it had hoses coming out of it.

On the end of the hoses there was a mouth piece
you would breathe into.

When I got there I had to take all my clothes
off and put on a hospital gown. I even thought that
was strange at the time even at five years old. I
remember it being so cold and the pillow was hard.
The nurse would put a sheet over me and tell me to
be quiet. I would lay there for hours it seemed
like. Sometimes Mother would read to me and
sometimes I would drift off to sleep, but I was
always uncomfortable and always cold. After a
long time Dr. Watson would appear and he would
ask Mother to wait outside. He would roll the
basal metabolism machine over and put the hoses
into my mouth. The mouthpiece was large for a
little girl, and it hurt, but he was never kind. He
would just tell me to breathe and he would turn the
machine on . He would then go to the end of the
table and pull up the sheet and force himself into
me. I never saw anything but his face, but the

mean, intense look on his face scared me to death. I didn't know what was happening to me, I just knew fear and incredible pain. I remember how I was afraid to cry because I thought he would hurt me even more, if that was possible.

I remember how skinny and bony he was. He always had his white coat on, a white shirt and grey trousers, and for being so skinny he had a little paunch that looked funny at the top of his trousers. He always wore his stethoscope and it was tucked into his shirt. He never said anything to me but, "breathe!" I was so in pain the tears would finally flow down my little face and after he was done raping me he would take tissue out of one of those small boxes they keep in doctor's offices, and wipe me off, wipe off his hands, come over and take the graph paper off the machine, pull the hoses out of my mouth. He would leave the room and never say a word.

Mother would come into the room and get me dressed. She knew nothing and the nurses never had to be in the exam rooms in those days. I was in shock. I didn't know what had happened, but after that first attack, after that day in 1951, I was never the same again.

I can remember preferring to be by myself from that time on. I know I knew something was very wrong, but I could never say anything to anyone.

In September of 1951 I became very ill, with a high fever. I was taken to Hillcrest Hospital again. I was very afraid, because my Mother called Dr. Watson and I could hear her conversation and my Daddy could not go with me as he had to stay and run the motel. Daddy had become my protector after the first attack and Mother even though she loved me deeply and in my mind I knew she did, but to my child-side I could not trust her. She did not know the real Dr. Watson and she

was the one who physically took me to his office. I know she never knew what he did, but in a way I felt she was at fault and that damaged our relationship. Mother again that night was the one to take me to the hospital to see Dr. Watson.

When we arrived at the hospital I was carried into the hospital by Marty's dad. I can remember being so glad to see him and so relieved that he was there. In my little mind he had to be like my Daddy and would keep me safe from Dr. Watson. I remember that vividly and I have told Marty about it and she said that her daddy remembers carrying me in and how scared I was looking into my big blue eyes.

I was so scared that night. I had been raped by the Dr. once and I thought it could happen again. I of course, did not know it was rape. I just knew fear and pain from this man, a man, a Doctor, who was to make you well, not destroy you.

That night I was diagnosed with polio. Marty's dad was at the hospital because he was on The March of Dimes committee with Mother, and they had just purchased a hot pack machine. The hot pack machine was developed right here in Minneapolis by Sister Kenny.

I was the first to use the hot pack machine in Silver City. I remember the bright lights of the hospital room, I was wrapped in these hot, wool, towels for the next twenty-four hours.

The nurses wrapped my arms and my legs and used huge safety pins to keep them tight. I remember how hot they were, but mostly I remember the smell of hot, wet wool. The heat was to stop the paralysis.

I was in the hospital for days. Mother was quarantined with me and my sister couldn't go to school. They had to burn her books for there was little known about polio then. I was so lucky as I had a mild form of polio and I didn't need braces,

but for months I was tested and measured to see if my arms and legs were growing properly.

Over the next two years I had numerous BMR tests and I would endure the attacks of Dr. Watson. I don't know if he raped me every time or not. It could have been as many as twelve times over two years. I just know from the scar tissue I have today, it was numerous times and always in that room in the basement in the old clinic on Cooper Street.

My childhood was over. I was no longer a happy free-loving child. I pretended to be, but I was emotionally destroyed. I buried the memory of those attacks deep in my mind.

When you are sexually abused as I was with no opportunity for therapy back in the fifties you live only by fear. You react on instinct of fear and what might cause that pain again. The only two feelings I had were fear and pain, until a year ago.

To me, men other than my Daddy, were powerful, they always had control and if you didn't please them you would be in pain. I felt helpless my whole life against men, because they were powerful, they always won, or got their way in the end.

I always liked men, but your mind does not work normally after severe sexual abuse. It is like a handicap of the mind. You are not crazy, you aren't a bad person but part of you never grows up. You can't process things like normal people do. Part of your mind process stays child-like. Partly because you want to forget the horror and your mind is protecting your sanity. Partly your mind is frozen in time, it remains and reacts like a child.

Part of my mind stopped when Dr. Watson started raping me. That is why there were fantasies and unrealistic promises and even lies. A child will say anything to avoid punishment. That

part of my brain never grew up until I remembered so many years later.

There are so many others like me and the sad thing is that abuse is preventable. It is a learned act, not like a disease or a birth defect. It isn't pretty, it is violent and a child like I was is powerless against the abuser. You have no choice. Your rights are taken away and the pain is almost too much to bear. That is why so many survivors of abuse bury the memory for years and years and it takes another shock or another painful event to trigger the memory.

When I started remembering, my life opened like a book. I could see how my life choices were made on fear. I can still feel fear at times, but now I can get it in perspective. I can tell you how I wanted to die sometimes in my life because not only did I hate myself I hated my choices. I never felt in control of my life until I remembered. But you Stephen, somehow after we met in high school

you always made me feel special, you made me feel worthy and I had never felt that in my life. Your kindness to me and Michael's devotion saved my life.

It has been a horrible struggle to remember and Michael has given up so much for me, but I think he knows one thing about me and that is that I love him even with all my struggles. I know there were days he wanted to run, to leave, but he had no place to go. He hated me sometimes and I hated everyone sometimes. I hated all the lies I lived with and the lies everyone told to protect me.

What was so bad about my past even with the rapes that nobody who loved me could tell me the truth? The lies and secrets are what almost destroyed me, not the truth.

After I started first grade I was hiding behind a fantasy world. I was gaining weight at a rapid pace. I went from 60 pounds to 100 pounds in a year and a half. I pretended that school was

okay and I was always smart enough to get good grades, I was never disruptive in a classroom. I wanted to please and make everyone happy and then I would be happy, and feel love and nobody would hurt me.

I was different from all the other kids and I knew, I knew more about life. I always felt old. Maybe not old, but wise about life. The only place I ever felt safe was at home with Daddy and Mother but especially Daddy. I would follow him around like a shadow and we were always close.

I always remember fear and maybe that was because of the adoption too, but nobody would ever discuss it with me. Everything was better hidden or unspoken in those days. I was terribly distressed. I would fall asleep at the dinner table at night and Daddy would carry me to bed. I could forget about everything when I was asleep. Other than home, my bed was the safest place for me.

My stuffed animals always protected me. Looking back now, after I would endure a session with the Dr., that night, I would take my sleeping bag, summer or winter, and zip myself inside my bed, in my sleeping bag, with my normal covers on top of me and my stuffed animals surrounding me. My animals protected me, and they never hurt me. Mother would get so upset and say I would get too hot and burn up, but I didn't care. I would refuse to get out, and I would sleep that way for several nights until I felt safe again in my mind. Everyone thought I was nuts I'm sure.

I would take my anger out by tearing things apart. I remember Mother saying that she bought me more Mickey Mouse watches because I would destroy them. By second grade I had gained more weight and I endured the jabs the kids made of being "fatso" and always being the last one picked for a team, but I didn't care. The name calling was

nothing compared to the pain I endured at a young age.

The reinforcement was there every day of my life that I was different from normal kids and that I was bad. The self-destructive behavior had begun in my eating habits to keep people away and especially men. I was such a good little kid. I was good and I was kind and I did anything anyone would ask of me, but it didn't matter how good or kind or helpful I was I never felt like I pleased anyone. I always felt bad or "tarnished" or un-equal to anyone.

My second grade teacher was different than any teacher I had had. She was a friend of my Grandparents so I saw her on a social level and at school. I could tell she never liked me. Most of my teachers did, but not her. She always wore lots of make-up and jewelry and tight knit dresses. I always thought she didn't like me because I was fat.

At the end of the school year in May, the PTA had a school carnival and the second graders got to do the May Pole Dance. The girls wore these pastel dresses and the boys wore pastel shirts with their jeans and of course I was too fat to fit in a dress.

Mother was always trying to make my life okay for me, so I did know she loved me. She contacted the lady who made the dresses and Mother was going to pay the dressmaker to make a dress for me, but the teacher wouldn't let Mother and wouldn't let me be in the program. I was crushed. Mother never forgave the teacher for that. I hid my feeling to make Mother feel better and told her it was no big deal but I didn't go to the carnival that year or any other year I was in grade school.

I remember that evening of the carnival, I got in my jeans and tennis shoes and I climbed up the hill behind the Pueblo Court where we lived. I

was always going off by myself. Silver City was very safe and it was late spring so it was not dark. I could see the grade school and the front yard of the school and I saw all my classmates dance around the May Pole. I stood there and cried. I knew then, for sure, that there was something about me that people didn't like. That my birth mother had given me away because there was something bad about me. Dr. Watson hurt me because I was bad and you know Stephen,until a year ago when I uncovered the truth about my past I always felt somehow, somewhere, something was bad about me, that I could never really be loved.

The third grade was no different than any other, except I had a nicer teacher. Every Tuesday or Wednesday the school nurse would visit North Silver Elementary. Our third grade class room was right by the front door with windows facing the front of the school. She would come right after lunch, and every week I would get sick like clock-

work and insist that the nurse call Mother or Aunt Gladys to come and get me. I was terrorized by her uniform and if she was there, surely the Dr. would be soon and I wasn't sticking around to find out.

My parents thought I was trying to get out of my piano lesson because it was on the same day that this would happen. I wasn't! Mother never did solve the problem. I liked my piano lessons, just not the selections of music the Catholic Sisters at St. Mary's made me play.

All through grade school if I ever knew the school nurse was coming to the school, I can remember the fear and feeling sick.

The rest of my grade school years were not any different from any other young girls. I was no longer being attacked. That stopped at seven when my original medical records show the last BMR exam.

I had wonderful friends like Danielle, who I started kindergarten with and Marty and Sam and Jenny. We went to Brownies and Girl Scouts and had slumber parties and went to movies and generally had fun. Daddy would let us use Room 15 at the Pueblo Court for our slumber parties a lot of the time. I'm sure we gave Daddy fits, but he would do anything I wanted.

My memories of Dr. Watson were vague, by then. I never liked the man, he was cold and in all the years he never looked me straight in the eyes, ever.

My childhood was gone as far as I can remember. I pretended to be carefree and happy and yes we always had everything as far as material things. We had all the clothes and all the food to eat, a place to live and plenty of toys to play with. Both Ann and I were indulged, but I never for one minute was not grateful for all the advantages that I had and I knew I was blessed to have the parents

I was given. My memory of anything bad that had happened to me was totally gone and yet I always felt curious and unsettled about my past. I did not know the story of how my parents got me. I was adopted and that was that. The details were never revealed. I always felt so responsible and always grown-up. I could rent rooms at the motel at an early age and I could do the laundry and clean the rooms when the maids did not show up. Ann could do the same. As I said before I always felt grown-up.

At thirteen, just as I felt more in control of my own life, Daddy was stricken with a stroke and life changed again. Of course I didn't plan it and I didn't want anymore adult responsibility. I wanted to be more carefree like my friends seemed to be.

I really think the fragility of life was instilled in me while Daddy recovered from his stroke, because I saw him come so close to death's door. The Dr. even told me at that time, that once

the stroke process begins, that there are always more strokes. It might take years, but the odds that Dad would die from a massive brain hemorrhage were great. Daddy was the man who protected me from harm so this news was startling to me. From that time in 1959 I cherished each day I had my Dad in my life.

Stephen I can't really remember when we first met. It was either my sophomore or junior year at Silver High . I never had a boyfriend in high school because of my weight and that was okay with me. There were always group parties and dances and I was friends with both girls and boys. Oh, I had crushes on some guys but it was mostly in my own mind and that was fine. I was too busy helping at the motel and working with Dad on his therapy that dating was never an issue. There was always Danielle who broke up with her boyfriend weekly, or Marty's boyfriend was busy,

so I always had someone to do something with. We were all just one group of friends.

My sister had gone off to college in 1961, so I was really the one who got a lot of attention from my folks.

The first time I remember you was in Spanish class. Marty was in our class and a few others. But you sat in front of me and had wide shoulders. Your blue eyes were intense and your smile would melt anyone in a second.

We started talking and we were very much alike right in the beginning. Neither of us had much time for school work. School was a social event not a learning experience. I could have had straight A's and that really bothered Mother, but straight A's would have taken too much time and that was not for me. Remember how we traded our homework? One day you would do it and the next day I would. It worked perfectly, and Mr. Steele was never the wiser.

Remember when Marty's mother gave him a bottle of scotch and he upped Marty's grade? If we had only known that in the beginning. My Dad in the liquor business and the motel business we could have all had straight A's for a few cases of scotch and never done homework in Spanish Class.

Stephen, I did think about you and what it would be like if we were ever a couple, but you were always dating someone in your class. I enjoyed just being your friend and we would talk for hours on the phone or sit in the car and listen to the radio and talk. We both liked music and you had even started your own band and would practice in the basement of your house.

I was afraid or uncomfortable to ever go into your house. I didn't remember then why. I remember being in the living room once by the fireplace and then a few times in the basement where you practiced with your band. Marty and I would come over and listen to you play. We were just

very close friends and could always talk to each other.There was never anything more.

During high school I had health problems and weight problems. I would go to see Dr. Watson for a regular exam and my weight would be the issue. Of course I used my weight to keep me safe. I was on every diet in the book and it was a family topic. J.C. needs to try this diet, or that diet. I know everyone was concerned about my health but it really hurt my feelings after awhile.

As far back as 1959 Dr. Watson had me on a powerful amphetamine called Dexamyl. So for five years I was on drugs, addictive drugs to hype me up to loose weight. By 1963 I had energy all the time, but other medical problems started to surface. I would hemorrhage all the time from my period and I would never stop unless I was given shots every day. Mother would give me the shots and that didn't even work after awhile. Then Dr.

Watson put me on Enovid the first birth control pill and Librium as a tranquilizer.

I remember that I was either very happy or very sad. I was part of the drug culture and didn't even know it! Nobody questioned Doctors back then, you just took what they prescribed and they were the authority.

In the spring of my junior year and your senior year we were very close. You could tell me anything and I could tell you anything. It was so easy to talk to you and you were always so nice to me. One Sunday night we were in my car in front of your house, we were talking and you had on your red and black leather football jacket and you just leaned over and kissed me for a long time.

I was surprised but I liked it. We never discussed it after that. It was time for the prom and you were going steady with your girlfriend and I had a date with a friend.

I was Prom Chairman that year and the theme was "Sayonara"! I laugh about that name today, but it was special and romantic then.

The gym was decorated fabulously and we had the most wonderful band from Tucson, which was my idea. They were called The Persuaders, I think, and it took a huge chunk of our prom budget to hire them, but we did and Daddy gave them a room free at the Pueblo Court as part of the deal. I remember we danced together and you were so impressed with the band, and I felt really good that night. The prom was a huge success. That was 1963.

You graduated in the spring and moved to Las Cruces with your grandparents and I never thought I would see you again, and I did have a crush on you, but then who didn't. You were great looking, tall, a football player and nice besides. I knew my senior year would be so different without you to talk to.

Later that summer Marty's family got the foreign exchange student for our senior year and so we of course had to have a welcome party. I was really into entertaining by then so we planned a luau in my Grandparent's backyard in August, just before school started. They lived at 1809 Yucca Drive.

Jenny and Mandy and I hosted the party, but we needed a band. I called your mother to get your phone number because I knew you would know of a band we could get. You never even questioned what I needed, you said you would bring the band up to Silver, your own band, and you wouldn't even consider charging us. You said your band needed the practice. I could still count on you, you were still my friend. I knew you cared about me and I about you, but we were still too shy to say anything.

The party was exciting and your band played late. Everyone had a good time and nobody

wanted the party to end, especially me. Later after all the guests had left, you asked me to go for a ride. It was late and I knew my mother would have a fit because she was getting more over protective all the time. I had no intention of saying, "no" to you no matter what Mother said.

You and I could always talk and that night was no exception. We both felt alive again and free, and we were together. We talked and laughed and we both knew the night was going to end, but not yet. There was always an unspoken bond between us. We could always say anything to each other and the other one would understand. You didn't have to speak that night, but you did. You said, "I wish I could steal you away forever tonight." I agreed, but in my heart and reality as best I knew reality at that time, I knew your wish could never be.

I knew you cared about me and you knew that night that I cared about you. I always knew

that someday I would look into your blue eyes and see your smile and feel your warmth again.

Stephen, you were my first love, and I knew that at seventeen.

I graduated from Silver High School in May of 1964 and I went off to college in the fall.

Daddy had no more strokes at the time and he could shave and write and could pretty well handle the business again. I was always lucky Dad and Mother were so close and devoted to each other because they had a fabulous love between them. She was so strong and he was gentle and they just balanced each other so well. They were a team and it showed. They were never too affectionate in public, but Daddy would always kiss mother if she was going somewhere and they were always good to everyone. Lots of people in Silver City took advantage of their goodness and they didn't care. Mother and Dad were only happy doing for others. They had a comfortable life

style. After Daddy's illness finances got really tight, but they always managed somehow to give us what we needed.

Some of the best times I remember with Daddy were when we would get up early and go to Schadel's Bakery. Mr. Schadel would let Daddy put icing on the cake doughnuts and Daddy liked his sweets so the chocolate frosting was thick. He would get two glazed doughnuts for Mother and a plate of cake ones for Ann and I and himself.

Sometimes I would go to the barber shop with Daddy and he would always give me the change in his pocket for gum. Daddy even bought a red, Dodge truck, because I loved the color red.

My parents were always active in the city and Dad was on the city council. Early every morning you could smell the coffee downstairs. He always got up early and let Mother sleep. Daddy died over twenty years ago but I still miss his biscuits for breakfast and the fact that he was

so independent, but so caring. He would even fix breakfast for some of the salesmen who stayed at the Pueblo Court for years and were regulars.

I can remember Mother telling me how much she liked your grandfather and that he sold Pennzoil to them when they first came to Silver in the thirties from Arizona. Your grandfather and Daddy and a few other fellows would always have dinner when he was in town. That was before you and I, Stephen were even born.

If someone was sick Mother was the first to fix a custard or to get a ham baked for the family. That is all I ever knew on the great side of my childhood, and thank goodness they never had to know about what really happened to me.

Just before I went off to college I remember I really wanted red luggage and Mother was so conservative and she just didn't understand that, but my Aunt Gladys said,"For God sakes Elma let her have red luggage." I got red luggage and I still

have red luggage even some of the pieces from college. When I like something I like it forever.

I never saw Dr. Watson again after I went to college, but I was no longer on drugs prescribed by him. By then my past was buried so deep there was no way I would remember for years and years.

The only time I saw a doctor in college I had a annual pelvic exam and the Dr. told me I probably would never get pregnant because I had so much scar tissue. That is all he said and I didn't think too much of it because my mind had buried all the trauma I had as a child.

After I graduated from college I had no idea what I wanted to do, so I went to graduate school for the fall semester. That fall after I graduated my sister Ann called one day and said Grandmother had been talking and had told her the story of me arriving one night wrapped in a green army blanket at Aunt Glady's house.

I always knew I was adopted as I said before, but this was a new story to me. Ann tried to get Grandmother to say more, but she would not. I guess I had always assumed I was adopted out of the hospital like Ann, nobody ever said any different. That was when I thought maybe Dr. Watson was really my father. Years later I confronted Mother but she said, "that is the most ridiculous thing I have ever heard." It was at that point I knew she knew a lot more, but would never reveal it to me. I had heard all the stories about his life and I just figured I was another mistake of his.

Aunt Gladys would tell me all the gossip in town when we would visit together and we would laugh and then she would tell me not to tell my Mother what she had told me, it was our secret. I knew a lot about everyone and I felt a special closeness to my Aunt and she to me. It was like she would stand up for me and my opinions.

She was the one who kept me safe the first
night of my life, so there was a bond. Of course I
was such a curious kid that I thought one day she
would slip and tell me about me, but she never did.
I honestly believe my Aunt Gladys would have
told me if she had known. Everyone seemed to
protect everyone but she would have told me.
By January 1969 I was home finished with my
college life. I did not want to be a teacher like my
sister,who was teaching in California.

I had studied fashion and clothing and tex-
tiles and marketing. I wanted to work for a department store which Mother again did not like, but
she loved me, and figured by then I was determined, I would do it.

I interviewed with Macy's in San Francisco,
but I really didn't want to live that far from home
as Daddy and his health were still a concern for
me.

Marty and Sam and Jenny were all married by then and Danielle was teaching school at Cobre High School and living at home again to save some money. Danielle and I did things together when she wasn't dating her boyfriend from college. He was a place kicker in football and in April of that year he was drafted by the Houston Oilers. Danielle was dating all the time and she was hard to keep track of but we had been friends since we were five so we were close. Funny thing we still are and talk at least once every few months.

Marty was married and expecting her first baby in February and was living in Silver while her husband finished college at Western. So I had close friends around while I made a career decision.

I had been home just one week and I was in the office of the Pueblo Court. Daddy had gone upstairs to get something. I heard a yell and I ran

to the stairway as Daddy was falling head first
down the stairs. I caught him and stopped his fall
or his head would have hit the tile floor and he
would have been killed. He had cuts and bruises
and his head was bleeding in my lap. I screamed
for Mother and she came and called the ambulance
to take Daddy to the hospital. I had to stay at the
motel.

Daddy had a massive stroke that day and
when I got to the hospital he was sitting in a
wheelchair with tears rolling down his face he
said, "I don't want to be an invalid the rest of my
life!"

Here was a man who had been active and
independent, so giving and happy. He had fought
back from one stroke and now he knew he had lost
it all. I could hardly stand it, but I would do anything for this man I called Daddy. Daddy never
walked again.

Somehow I had come home at the right time and I knew then how much I meant to Mother. We had Daddy in the hospital, both my Grandmother and Aunt Gladys had had heart attacks and were recuperating at my Grandmother's home. We had a maid taking care of them around the clock. My cousin was two months away from having her second baby in Anthony, New Mexico and Mother and I had the Pueblo Court to run and the Gem Liquor Store and be at the hospital with Daddy as often as possible. By summer we really had every-thing under control.

Daddy was home getting therapy every day, but he could not walk and we had to hire help to lift him and bathe him, but we did everything else. I shaved him every day while he was in the hospi-tal and when he came home.

Mother knew then how strong and capable I was, but I had a great example. She was tough and demanding and her way was the only way, but she

was always there if I needed anything and it would not be too many years until I really needed her.

I was getting really restless to get started on my career and I was getting very bored in Silver City. I had contacted Goldwaters in Phoenix and I was going into their buyer's training program in August of 1969. Danielle and I were going to move to Phoenix together as she wanted to get on her way too. We made a trip to Phoenix , rented an apartment and she got a job in the Scottsdale School System. That was the fourth of July week-end.

When we got home that weekend I had a letter from Goldwater's telling me that I didn't have a job that they were only going to train people that already worked for them. I was furious and so Mother suggested I call the personnel director back and get some answers. I had an apartment and no job. Well the lady at Goldwater's suggested I call the personnel director at Diamond's

Department Store named Don. I did and that was the best thing that had happened to me in a long time.

I was in his office in Phoenix two days later and that was a Monday. He hired me immediately. I returned home to pack and I was a trainee working on the floor by Thursday of that same week.

That was the first time I had really felt accomplishment with self esteem and I was happy and challenged knowing exactly the career I wanted as a buyer for a major department store was within reach. I will always feel grateful to Don for giving me my first chance and to the parent company of Diamond's, the Dayton-Hudson Corporation.

That was over twenty years ago and they are still believing in the future of people and are one of the most socially responsible corporations today. That choice of career was the first real choice I had ever had in my life.

All I cared about after I went to work for Diamond's was my career during the week and then I would go to Silver City every weekend to help Mother with the business and Daddy.

Daddy would be so happy to see me and it was a lift for him after his long tedious weeks in therapy and his frustration at not being able to do anything but sit or lay down and watch TV.

I loved being with Daddy, and Mother would get a little break when I was home. I also felt very safe there. I didn't realize I was avoiding social situations by going home every weekend.

I dated one guy one time and I remember I couldn't get home fast enough. I was simply frightened and I couldn't explain why. It was not being uneasy, it was fear.

I could have plenty of social life with my salesmen as I was a buyer within a year of going to work for Diamond's. I would fly to New York to market and L.A. and I was treated royally wher-

ever I went. I was always in a business atmo-
sphere with other buyers so I was never afraid.

I was happy and I was thinner than I had
ever been. I would get up at four in the morning
and go to the masseuse and then have a steam bath
and I would eat only protein and water, and I felt
fabulous. I was happy professionally and I felt in
control of my life, but I wasn't at all.

A couple of years had past and Mother and
Dad sold the motel, Grandmother and Aunt Gladys
had both died and I talked Mom and Dad into
moving to Phoenix so Dad would be closer to
medical facilities. He had visited Barrows Neuro-
logical Institute, earlier in the year and had felt a
lot better, but he was still having little strokes.
They finally moved and they bought a beautiful
townhouse and I moved in with them so I could
help Mother with Daddy as he needed around the
clock care by then.

Danielle had married the June before, not to the football player, but to a wonderful guy she met in Phoenix.

It was then that I started getting close to Peter, who was also employed by Diamond's. He was older and successful and I think he was attracted to my mind and the enthusiasm I had for the retail business. I was also wanting to date and be with men. I wanted to feel normal, but I just wasn't. I had always stayed away from that part of my life. I liked men and I was just so shy and afraid and I did not know why.

Peter and I were dating secretly for a long time and of course I was really beginning to explore my sexuality. Everyone was sleeping with their boyfriends and I was thinking I was in love with Peter. Perhaps he was a father image to me as I knew Daddy's health was getting more fragile. He was giving me lots of attention and I had a fantastic life style.

I wanted to know what sex was like and yes I had always been taught to not sleep with anyone but the man you marry, but I always had felt like I was "tarnished" and maybe I even felt worldly. There was always something in the back of my mind saying I was bad anyway, so what difference would it make. I certainly wasn't sleeping with everyone I met, in fact I hadn't slept with anyone yet.

One night I got drunk and had sex with Peter. I wanted to be normal for once in my life. My fears were gone with the liquor and I'm sure Peter thought I was a virgin and I certainly thought I was a virgin, but I wasn't and I had never slept with anyone as far as I knew. I was shocked and Peter was shocked. So that was just another bad thing about me I thought.

My mother confronted me about sleeping with Peter and I told the truth, but I wished I hadn't. I think I wanted her to say J.C. its okay, I

still love you, but lets rethink where you are taking your life. She never did. I felt like she thought I was a hooker. I was a fallen woman and yet neither of us knew the real truth about my virginity.

In June of 1972 Daddy had a massive stroke and died six hours later. He was the person I had trusted my whole life and he was gone. I was glad he no longer had to lay in bed on his back, but I still miss him terribly. Daddy was more than special he respected his wife and his daughters and anyone he knew. He was gentle and loving and a friend to all. He was one of a kind.

A month later I had no choice, but to get Peter to marry me. Luckily he was transferred to Oklahoma City and he had never lived anywhere but Phoenix. He didn't love me and I didn't love him but we needed each other and I certainly didn't feel safe with Mother and I didn't know why.

Mother moved back to Silver City. I wanted to have a wedding like my friends had had, but she said she would not give me a wedding if I married Peter, so I knew I was alone again.

Daddy was gone and I had to do what I had to do. I arranged my own wedding with the help of Peter's sister and brother-in-law. We were married by a justice of the peace because the Rabbi wouldn't marry us because I wasn't Jewish. I had a white long dress and beautiful flowers and I was married, and I was determined to make it work.

It took a year before Mother would even write a letter to me addressed in my married name. I would hide the letters from Peter so his feelings would not be hurt. Mine were hurting enough. Finally after a year I guess she figured she either had to accept my decision or not have me, as unhappy as she was. In the end she tried her best and Peter tried his best, but I was always the one in the middle keeping everyone happy.

Peter and I had absolutely nothing in common, but loneliness and retailing. I always hid my real feelings and yet we did get along pretty well but we didn't laugh and we never did anything but work at Peter's career from morning until night.

I was determined to be the perfect wife and nobody would ever suspect I was in so much pain on the inside. I would never blame Peter because we were both hiding a lot of pain and unhappiness and we did not know how to have a relationship at all. I would never confront any issue and neither would Peter. I was too afraid from my past, a past I had no memory of. I would keep the peace at any cost. Anything to keep Peter happy.

Three years into the marriage I got pregnant and I was shocked especially because I had been on birth control pills and never expected I could get pregnant. I guess Peter and I had a normal sex life. I think I encouraged a lot of sex to please Peter and to keep Peter calm and relaxed and I

thought that is what all men wanted and I was great at pleasing.

I remember when I called Peter at work and I told him I was pregnant the only thing he said was "J.C. you are going to get an abortion aren't you?" There was no question it was a command. That day my heart sank and Peter lost his wife for good. He didn't care about me at all and that was my confirmation. That was Peter, he wanted all the good things in life but did not know how to nourish a personal life, he just had no time for anything but his career and his well being. That is fine if you are not married. Then I called my Mother and told her and she was even less thrilled. God, all I thought was why can't someone some time in my life be thrilled for me. Be happy that I'm happy.

Well I went to the abortion clinic on Roberts Street in Oklahoma City and I was sick. God had given me a chance to have a baby and not Peter not anyone was going to take my baby from me. I had

lived my whole life and I was almost thirty years old and I had never known a biological mother and this baby was my own flesh.

I was scared to death, but I left the clinic and I went home and told Peter I was too far along to have an abortion and I didn't care.

I hated Peter and I hated Mother for not wanting my baby. Of course after I had Michael everyone thought he was wonderful, but I always knew he was.

I had Michael by caesarean section because his neck was caught and he couldn't drop into the birth canal. After he was delivered late one night, I woke up in the recovery room the next morning, Peter was in a meeting at the store, but Mother was at my side. I opened my eyes and I said, "I'm sorry I didn't have a girl." Mother had wanted a granddaughter. I was so into pleasing everyone that I apologized for something I had no control over.

I regret my Daddy never knew Michael but Mother turned out to be the perfect Grandmother for Michael and they had a wonderful relationship. The last time they were together they sat close on the sofa at Ann's house. Mother had Parkinson's disease so she had a hard time walking, she was almost blind, but they sat for hours and Mother told Michael all about the time when the bomb was exploded at White Sands so many years ago and many other stories he asked about. He could ask her anything and she would tell him, He loved her so much and she him.

The fact that I lived with a man who never considered my feelings amazes me now. I don't blame Peter for it, I blame myself. I was afraid and I based everything I did on those fears and I made totally wrong decisions. I will always be grateful to Peter, for the fact that without him I wouldn't have Michael and he is worth everything.

I never took birth control pills again and I never got pregnant again.

Peter and I divorced after fifteen years of marriage. I had totally died inside by that time and I had destroyed myself. I had gained a tremendous amount of weight, I'm sure trying to get Peter to hate me as much as I hated myself.

After I filed for divorce I had a call on New Years Day 1986 from Marty and Sam. We had all kept in touch and they were really worried about me, so they told me to get rid of Peter and Michael for Valentine's weekend they were coming to visit. They got Danielle and the three of them came and it was like we had never been apart. I realized that I was living a total lie and had for years. There was no love in my marriage, just neediness and I felt like a maid and a hooker. We never laughed.

Peter always blamed me and hated me sometimes for breaking up his perfect life, but it

was as fake as anything and it was time to try to put a life back together.

Peter was always so hard on himself, I guess we both were, but he is one of the most creative men I've ever known and brilliant in his field of Cosmetics. I don't care how hard you try divorce is horrible for everyone involved.

People forget that we are human and we all make mistakes. Strength comes in recognizing our mistakes, correcting them and doing better. The problem with that is, that so many of us have tried to please others for so long, that we forget about our own well being and feel that whatever we do we are wrong.

Stephen, during some of the lonely times, through all those years, I did wonder where you were, but I never really thought you cared about me so I dismissed the thoughts.

Michael and I moved back to Minneapolis after my divorce, as I couldn't face the guilt I felt

every day for taking Michael away from his father. I also knew the schools better and I had a good support system in Minnesota. Michael thrived and was happy and I seemed to be too.

I was still trying to please Mother and I had her move to Minneapolis with us as Michael was her only grandchild. She had stopped driving in Silver City and her health was not the best and I for one deep inside did not trust the Doctors or the medical facilities in Silver City. I still didn't know why.

I met new friends like Savannah who was divorced with two sons and Zellie, whose husband had died a few years before and her children were raised. I was really at peace, I thought, but I wasn't at all. I was still taking care of everyone but myself.

Finally Mother's health was more than I could even handle. She was becoming almost neurotic about going to the Doctor. Every pain

was something major and she was so nervous every time Michael and I left the house. It was getting too stressful for Michael and I. We could not have any kind of a normal life.

I had been asked to join the Soccer Board in Edina and that was good for me and Michael as he loved playing soccer goalie and I had a chance to meet emotionally healthy men in a non-threatening situation.

I met Carin and Bob and so many more wonderful friends that went out of their way for me.

I still had no desire to date like Savannah did or any other of my single friends. Yes, I think I needed time to recover from the emotions of a divorce, but that wasn't it. I was afraid, and not normal afraid. I was fearful of my well-being. I never felt safe.

I had put Mother in a rest home with her own room so she had people around, had her meals

served, so she didn't forget to turn the stove off
and if she fell like she did so often there was someone who checked on her all the time. I thought I
did the right thing, but Mother wanted me there all
the time and so I felt guilty about that. Everyone
our age goes through having aging parents and it is
really hard to keep your emotions in check and live
your own life.

I had to get a new career going. I could not
go back into retailing as it had changed so much
and I had been away for so many years. Yes, I
kept up with it through Peter and all the papers,
and figures and layouts I did to help him, but that
does not relate to a strong resume.

I decided to get my real estate license and I
did. My life was about to take a turn to the past. I
think I was already starting to find the real truth
hidden deep in my mind.

I had been divorced for three years, It was a
hot August afternoon. I had just picked up

Michael from his tennis lesson and we were going out to start buying school clothes later. I ran into the house and the phone was ringing off the hook. The air conditioning was not working and that was just another minor problem that had plagued my life since I got divorced. The last three years had been hard financially and emotionally and I was ready to finally get a break in life. But at this point I thought I never would. I remember thinking, "please don't be Mother calling from the rest home to tell me one more bizarre tale she was hallucinating about. I couldn't take anymore today." She would call me about people under her bed, people doing horrible things, she was afraid. Maybe she was struggling to keep the past in the past and her fear was overwhelming to her. I don't know.

Picking up the phone and falling on my bed I said, "Hello." To my surprise it was Samantha calling. Thank goodness a friendly voice on the other end. Samantha asked me if I was sitting

down and she starts telling me that she and Mark were getting divorced after twenty years of marriage. I think I told her I could believe it, because the weekend in 1986 when we were all together I had picked up on an incident and I knew she had experienced what I had in my marriage. Now the third friend had done the same thing we all had done. J.C., Sam and Marty all born the same month, the same year, grew up in the same town, married for some other reason but love, and all had troubled marriages and now we were all out of them,or about to be in Sam's case.

Sam went on to explain that after she and Mark had decided to divorce that Rob had called. I remembered the name, but didn't know why, it had been so long ago. Rob was Sam's boyfriend in college, but Sam's dad didn't like Rob and broke them up. Now Sam was telling me that she and Rob would be married after her divorce. How was this all happening, but I knew Sam was in love and

I was thrilled for her. I hung up the phone that day happier than I had been in years, knowing that my other friend Sam would finally be happy. Marty had found the love of her life after I married Peter and had been so happy. Now again it was me who was alone, but I really didn't care and I really never gave it a second thought.

I had to get Michael raised and get my new career going and take care of Mother as best I could, who had time to think about love. Michael and I went shopping that evening and I smiled all evening thinking about Sam and Rob. Finally together after all these years.

I was getting ready for work the next morning, when Marty called to see if I had heard from Sam and we laughed and we shed some tears because divorce is not happy and we had grown up with Mark and we had both been in Sam and Mark's wedding. But we knew what we had all been through together. Marty told me that she had

gone to a class reunion a few weeks before. It was for three classes from Silver High. I knew about it, but I was not that thrilled to go back to Silver City. I loved my friends from there, but I never felt comfortable with the town, no matter what people would say. I passed on the reunion, but for some reason, out of the blue, I asked her if you were there Stephen. That you were the only other person I had ever wondered about, except of course she and Danielle and Jenny and Sam, but we all kept in touch. Marty said, "no". She knew instantly that I still cared about you. Marty had had cancer a few years before and she taught us all how important today is and she said to me, "J.C., life is not a dress rehearsal, if you want to know something or where Stephen is then find him, call him!"

I went off to work and I thought about it later in the day and laughed and wondered why after all these years we had never crossed each

other's paths. It was fun to think about it and very romantic after listening to Sam's story the day before, but I was sure you were married and had a couple of kids and would never want to hear from me.

Later that night, Michael had gone off to a movie with friends I sat down at my desk and dialed information. I still wondered what I was doing trying to find you.

Would you even remember me as the operator gave me your number. I called the operator and asked the call be person to person just in case it was the wrong number. I had gone this far I was going to do it.

Suddenly my life flashed in front of me, and then I heard that voice that I knew so well. I asked you if you remembered me and you were shocked, but we talked for a long time that night catching up on the twenty-six years that we hadn't spoken. It was like we had never been apart. We closed by

giving each other our phone numbers and addresses and said we would keep in touch.

I couldn't sleep that night so I got up and wrote you a friendly letter, not a love letter and said that if Michael and I were ever in your area, we would love to take you to dinner. I sent the letter off the next morning, but I never imagined what would happen next.

Two days later the phone rang in the middle of the afternoon and it was you Stephen. You told me that you couldn't believe I was back in your life and you gave me your 800 number at the office to call you anytime and you would call me.

We questioned why we never tried to find each other and realized that neither of us thought the other ever cared, but we knew that we cared more than each of us had ever hoped. We parted exactly twenty-six years to the month from when we said good-bye in Silver City after your band had played for my party. We never knew if we

would ever look into each other's eyes again or if our lips would ever meet again and know the sweetness of our youth.

Stephen, I never would have called again without your encouragement because my whole history with men was untried really. I wasn't good at relationships and I knew I was mixed up from my life. Slowly but surely you made me feel safe and we laughed and encouraged each other to live our own life to follow our dreams so to speak. I was free and could do anything I wanted. We talked about being adults and not kids anymore, that we didn't have to please anyone anymore.

I remember the day I sold the first house in my career and I called to tell you and in a few hours a bouquet of flowers was delivered to my door, with a note, "Congratulations, Love, Stephen." Michael got home from school and knew they were from you. He was delighted be-

cause I was so happy. I still have that card and the other notes and letters you sent.

You would go into the office on Saturdays and call me and we were talking for hours on the phone. Monday nights when the guys were in the office watching Monday Night Football, you were telling me everything I ever dreamed of hearing. You told me you loved me and that you would take care of Michael and me forever, but that wasn't the way it would turn out. You were the most sensitive and romantic man I had ever met and we could tell each other everything and anything and we were happy. The only problem was that we were living a secret, a fantasy and the closer to a relationship we came the darker side of my past started surfacing and controlling me and my actions and what I said. We still cared about each other and I would do anything to please you, but you didn't want it that way. I was so afraid

you were too good to be true and I also believed I could never be loved.

Remember the day I sent you boxed lunches for you and your best friend. I had chocolate covered strawberries in yours that said the next time you had strawberries I would be feeding them to you. We were happy Stephen, we were in love, or I thought we were. Remember the poem I sent you for your birthday that year:

YESTERDAY-TODAY-FOREVER

Yesterday a smile a glance,
Youth in love was not a chance.
His eyes so blue, his smile so bright,
Her eyes would shine and sparkle at night.
The time they would share, they were never aware,
But the love the care was always there.
A break a distance, far apart,
Left these two friends with empty hearts.
As the years went by the thoughts were there,
Where was she, and did he really care?
The lonely nights, the hurt the pain,
Would true love really be in the game?
Why was life so hard, and so untame?

Would she be loved, or was it always the same?
His eyes were sad, the sparkle dim,
Where had his life really taken him?
Was there more or was there less?
Was his life not to be the very best?
Today, one call, a voice filled with care,
Could he believe, that she was really there?
The laugh was hers and he could hear,
She was never really gone, so what did he fear?
His heart was lighter, his smile began,
The happy conversations, the sharing once again.
Years ago in the night, why hadn't they known?
Yet the one kiss they shared, never left them alone.
Talking endless hours, making love in their dreams,
They confessed a bond together each had never seen.
The love they had found was meant to last,
It filled up their souls and erased the past.
Forever blue eyes shining, hearts joined again,
The path that they follow is about to begin.
Apprehensive and nervous, and sometimes shy,
A dream can come true for this girl and this guy.
For once in a lifetime, a rare love you see,
But twice is a gift, God meant their love to be.
                                        JC 1989

Stephen you were the one who encouraged
me to write, and you even called me one Thursday
to have dinner with you in a city we both knew

well. I never went and when you were to come to visit in Minneapolis I screwed that up too. We were too close and you were too perfect in what you said and that scared me. I would purposely cause problems create confusion, keep you off guard, push you away. That was my child-side that I was just beginning to meet. I could not tell you why I made up things, why I couldn't be straight and precise in my life, I just felt fear and I would do anything to keep pain away.

In my fantasy world I was sure that you loved me and that we would be together and yet you were hesitant and I know that my confusing behavior really changed our relationship. The problem was I didn't know what to do. I was even scaring myself sometimes with how confused I got.

Savannah in the beginning told me that she thought I should just go for it, because she thought we would be happy. She had seen me so unhappy

and now I was so happy. Carin wanted me to be happy, but she was much more cautious because she was afraid I was too generous and she is the one person who understood my fear. She and Bob were anxious to meet you and Bob had talked to you on the phone and you told him you would be here soon.

Savannah taught me that you look at things and see what is the worst thing that could happen. We would be enemies forever. Well even at the worst point I hope that didn't happen.

Savannah is about the most honest person I have ever known and she knows herself well. She knew how thrilled I was at being really in love and she was right, that feeling was worth everything to me.

I was determined to see you face to face and then I had to have surgery I had been putting off. But you seemed attentive to me again and I was definitely attentive to you. You sent me flowers

for my birthday, for Valentine's Day and there were flowers when I got home from the hospital. Carin called you to let you know I was okay and Michael called you too.

Two days after major surgery, Michael and I drove to see you. The trip was a long one, but I could recuperate at Martys' and Michael could get his driver's license. The month would do us both good.

You and I were to meet for the first time at the Scanticon Hotel. I made all the arrangements, and that was where I could shine. I had had lots of experience in that field all my life. I had the crystal goblets, Carin and Bob had sent out a bottle of Tattinger Champagne and I had ordered fabulous appetizers from a caterer. I had it arranged to perfection.

Michael was spending that weekend with his father and it was really the first time in years I had a free moment and I couldn't wait to see you.

After I got Michael settled with his father, I went back to the hotel. You called, but I told you not to come over until six-thirty. I wanted to have a bath and rest a little, it had been only a few days since I had major surgery and I still had stitches.

I put the champagne on ice and I dressed to perfection and I was a nervous wreck. I tried to call Savannah in Minneapolis, no answer. Then I called Carin and she told me to calm down. Then I went to the window and I started watching for you.

You drove up, and you walked across the parking lot. It was like seeing you walk down the hall in high school. It was only moments until you knocked on the door and I quickly opened it,to see you standing there. You hadn't changed. Yes the years were there, but your blue eyes sparkled, your smile was bright and those shoulders, still so wide. You were everything I could have imagined and more. We didn't know what to do, after twenty-seven years, the moment did not seem real.

It was real, and you opened the champagne and we laughed and talked and drank and ate. I'm sure some people thought we would sleep together, but we never did. We were sure we would wait until our lives were settled. The beauty about the love we had, was that it was based on a lifetime friendship. We shared, and we laughed and talked and we never did have to have a physical relationship to know how we really felt. The connection had been there. We were so easy with each other. We could almost predict what the other one was thinking.

That night when you left, you kissed me good-bye, and it felt as special as when you kissed me in high school. I couldn't believe you remembered that high school kiss, but you did.

Michael met you and thought you were great and the two of you talked for hours on every subject. It was all too easy and too good to be true.

At that point I saw you a few more times, we met in the Scanticon Hotel but our time together was over. It was too late for me, I was too afraid to trust you completely and all I did was confuse you and make problems. I had lost total control of my financial life, my personal self and everything I had. You were totally confused by me, but after that last night in November of 1990 when you walked me out of the hotel, I knew it was good-bye and that you had too many things to handle in your own life and I was just another bad, overwhelming problem. I never came through on any of the promises I made that day because I couldn't . I had lost control of everything, and I was too afraid to tell you.

You had already given me a lot of advice but I never really understood until much later. You were gone, and that feeling of attention and love was lost. I totally pushed you out of my life because I was too afraid. I was too programmed to

believe I was bad and in the end you would not be there anyway. I could point to the fact that we were never seen together by anyone but Michael, that you really didn't love me, but that was nonsense since I understood that in the beginning. I wanted to blame you and everyone else for my problems, but it was only me. I just needed time to reclaim my life, from the past and I hoped you would understand.

Remember how you encouraged me to find out about my adoption and I called Jim an attorney in Silver City who we went to high school with and he went to work and opened the records.

We had to petition the court to open the records and Lee the judge, wanted to know why I wanted to know who my birth parents were. I just thought Lee was another person in Silver City trying to keep me from uncovering all the lies. I told Jim to tell Lee, "that I wanted to know what

everyone in Silver City knew, that I didn't." The records were opened!

Jim faxed me the papers and when I got the file I was in shock. The records were in my Mother's handwriting, the Mother who adopted me and always told me she knew nothing. There was no attorney of record and there was no Dr. of record and only my birth mother's real name was listed. My father was unknown, which was common in those days. Mother always knew who I was and I always knew she did no matter what she said.

Quickly I contacted a few friends and yes I got all the answers and I even got a photo of my birth mother Jenny. Michael looks more and more like her everyday. He has her coloring and blue eyes and blondish brown hair. You saw her photo.

I also found out that she was already dead and that she hid the truth about me. It was Eddie's sister who I had always known. She filled in the story that wasn't in the adoption papers for me.

She told me that Jenny was a lovely lady, and she always wanted a daughter. She and Eddie lived a long time together and had two sons, one three years younger than me and one five years younger than me.

No, Stephen I have never contacted them. I gave my phone number and address to Eddie's sister but I never heard anything after the photo she sent. I suspected there was a lot more to the story than anyone told me and there was. My birth mother Jenny had a history of alcoholism and she had tried to commit suicide. She, I was told was never the same after the night they found her in the Bullard Hotel.

How could she be. She had given her baby away, she had lost the man she really loved and she married a man who she hadn't seen in years. She was a wonderful mother and wife I was told.

I am sure she saw me in Silver City, as she knew who adopted me and my parents lived a very

high profile life in the community. I was very sad to find out that she had already been dead about fifteen years. I really wished I could have met her and told her I loved her and I knew she loved me and did the only thing she could do in 1946.

It was also very strange that I could not tell my adoptive Mother, the only one I knew as Mother that I knew the truth. She never would understand, she would think I didn't love her, but I did.

There were some really different things about my birth certificate, different from my sister's who had been adopted three years before. My birth was never recorded until a year after I was born when the adoption papers were filed. Judge Marshall pretty much did whatever he wanted to do and he could cover up anything he wanted. My birth mother gave me the name I carry today and that really pleases me. Ann, my

sister's name was partially changed by our adoptive parents.

I had a hard time finding information about my birth dad and Eddie's sister gave me only a name to go on, but she wasn't sure if he was who Jenny was engaged to. It took me awhile, but I found the answer. I know now why even my birth mother, Jenny was treated like an outcast, even though nobody knew about her baby girl or that she was pregnant. She was treated wonderfully when she was engaged to Eddie, but she was left alone when she was in love and engaged to John.

So many questions came into my mind about my birth dad. Why would John give Jenny up, after all he loved her enough to get engaged to her? Why did I feel so different and I know I was treated differently growing up in Silver City than my sister was, who was a local adoption just like I was? My sister and I looked nothing alike, which is of course understandable, we aren't related. She

was blond and blue eyed. I was very dark haired and blue eyes and I was so different in personality in every way.

Oh, Stephen life is cruel sometimes and yet it is so predictable. I always knew something in my background just didn't fit. I had totally buried the memory of being sexually abused as a child and I didn't even discover that until years later when I married. No, I was different, I was treated differently in the family. I was over protected and I was almost treated with "kid gloves" as the expression goes. Yes, I was not healthy but I was treated differently.

As a little girl I could always see myself as I imagined in a huge picture of white fluffy sheep or baby lambs. Among all the white fluffy lambs there was one black fluffy lamb. She was sweet and kind and had a pink nose and a smile and four feet, but she was different from all the rest. Her coat was black.

You don't have to be a person of color or ethnic background or speak a different language. As a little girl I looked no different from the rest except my dark hair, but I was different to the few people who knew.

I was introduced to prejudice at a very young age. I didn't know I was experiencing that until recently when I put the whole story together. My adoptive parents knew, Dr. Watson knew and my birth mother, Jenny knew, and a few others in Silver City knew. It was unspoken always as it still is today, but it was there, and explains even more of my life.

My father John was Jewish. He was from one of the few Jewish families in Silver City.

In the forties, the time of Hitler, the Jewish families were hated for being Jewish, for being different. You didn't have to be in Germany, or New York or anywhere. You could be in Silver

City, or any small town and experience hatred. It is the same today.

A lot of Jewish families lived in fear from their past history and would not admit that they were of the Jewish faith. Some families in Silver City and other small towns changed their names or belonged to different churches and would hide. A lot of people today as in the past, live in a very ignorant state and believe that for some reason they are superior to others whether it is a religious difference, a race or ethnic difference or whatever it does not matter. There were Jewish families in Silver City that went to the Episcopal church and the Methodist Church and some families who were not so afraid to admit their difference, and would go as far away as Temple Mt. Sinai in El Paso, Texas for services on occasion. It took me almost two years to put the story together Stephen, but I did.

I could never understand, knowing myself so well by now, how my birth father gave up my birth mother when he loved her so much. He gave her up because he did love her and he knew that in the forties a Jewish man, married to a Catholic girl from West Texas was not going to be easy.

Oh, they would have married if Eddie hadn't returned. They would have made it because they were so in love. John only thought of Jenny, not of himself and let her go so she would not have the family conflicts he knew she would have. He gave her up so she would not have to suffer because of him, but she suffered anyway, and he never knew.

Jenny never named my father on the adoption papers to protect me from prejudice and give me a chance. She was trying to protect me. But I always knew there was a missing part to the puzzle. She did what she had to do, but she never forgave herself and she carried her sadness to her grave.

Dr. Watson knew who my father was and he was a totally sick man with how he treated woman including his wife and many of the women he destroyed with abuse. He left my mother to die as punishment for sleeping with a Jewish man rather than him. Thinking about John touching Jenny and not him was totally out of his realm of reasoning. He had all the power and felt he controlled everyone.

Dr. Watson saw me as my mother because I looked like her. I had her smile, her blue, blue eyes, but my father's dark, thick hair. It was pure power and hatred of Jews and his obsession with sex that drove him to rape me and rape me and rape me. I was nothing more than an animal to him and to me he was and is nothing less than Hitler.

All those years, all those hints, all those feelings I had were validated when I found out who my father was, and then I understood.

After you were gone out of my life and I
knew you didn't really love me I did want to die, I
wanted to give up and I wanted to stop the pain. I
wanted the truth about my life. Why I couldn't be
loved and have a relationship.

I know a lot of people gave up on me, including you, but my son never did and my sister
never did. Danielle and my friends in Minneapolis
never did. They protected me and gave me time to
recover from all the pain of my past. They didn't
push me and they never used me, they listened and
loved me.

Savannah was amazing, she just gave me
time to get myself back, no questions asked. Zellie
would call me all the time and we would talk over
coffee every weekend and she would listen and
listen and let me work my way out of the unreal
world I had put myself into. The world I had to
escape to in order to, protect my sanity and my
life, from the abuse I got from the Dr. as a child.

Zellie gave me the best compliment that I ever had. She said I was kind. According to Webster's definition it means sympathetic, friendly, gentle, tenderhearted, generous, cordial, loving, affectionate, natural and I think I am and I thank her for that.

I knew I was strong, you even said once that I was stronger than you, well I don't know, but I am strong enough to know that I never give up on me or my life or anyone that I love.

The morning I actually remembered the sexual assaults, I woke up startled and tears were flowing down my cheeks, just like I was five and I saw Dr. Watson at the end of the table and I knew who had raped me and where.

I was like I was laying in that room in the old clinic. I felt the hard table, I saw the room and I felt the coldness and I saw him. In remembering everything, I just knew that I was going to control

my own life and get rid of the fear that had plagued me always.

Finding you after all those years was a way for me to recover. You were the only safe person I knew from my past, and you would help me remember so I could find the truth and go on with my life. If I found out what totally messed up my life, I could have a successful relationship, I could find love and I could stop hating myself. I never wanted to hurt anyone, I just wanted the pain and loneliness and fear to stop.

Stephen, now you know. The old Watson Clinic on Cooper Street next to the courthouse was where I was raped as a child.

After Dr. Watson moved to his new clinic it was your father who bought the old clinic and converted it into a wonderful home for your family. Like I said before I was only in your house once or twice. I know now why I was always so uneasy about your house, but I didn't know then.

Isn't it interesting how many times our paths crossed but we never really got together.

Looking back now and seeing my life laid out like a map is sad at times, but I did have wonderful parents, all of them and I was so lucky to survive everything.

Mother always knew why I didn't get to do the May Pole dance in second grade it was not because I was fat, my teacher hated Jews. I found a letter written by my Grandmother's husband Roscoe who wrote about going to El Paso with this teacher and my Grandmother and her feelings were spelled out in the letter about how she felt about Jews. It made me sick. Top it all off Roscoe's father was a Jew but she didn't realize that.

When I was going to marry Peter and he was Jewish, I don't really think Mother hated that fact as much as she had always protected me from the fact of my heritage and she was afraid I would be hurt, not by Peter but by others who hated the

Jewish people. Mother even told me that she did not care how I raised Michael as long as he had a religious education. She enjoyed services the few times she went with me and Peter. I embraced the Jewish religion and Michael was raised in the Jewish faith. I always felt peace in the Temple and the Jewish faith is so family oriented that I loved it. I adored Peter's father and family. I felt more welcome in the Jewish faith sometimes than I did in the faith I was raised in because I always felt unclean in my own faith.

Peter and I were married by a justice of the peace as I said before because a Rabbi wouldn't marry a non-Jew. Peter and I were never invited to our neighbor's homes in Oklahoma City because Peter was Jewish, but I was always treated well and invited into homes because I was not Jewish. It took me years to figure that out. We lived eight years in the same house and were only invited into two homes ever. Some neighbors never even

spoke. It is almost comical how this all worked out. There is no rationale to hate and prejudice. It is just ignorance.

Stephen, you and I grew up in the southwest where we had best friends of different nationalities. I don't remember seeing a color or religion before I saw the person. I liked everyone and still do.

And for me well, I have put the past to rest other than I don't know if my birth father is still alive or not, but hope to find out soon.

I hope that you have forgiven me for any of the wrong choices I made. Once I found the truth it was so much easier to make the right decisions and I believe that the struggles I went through were for a reason.

I now feel like I'm looking down on another person's life, that the past is gone, I have finally, after all these years found me.

That fluffy black lamb in the picture in my mind is not bad anymore. She is unique and special and lovable and doesn't have to fear the mud that life throws at her, because her coat is black and the mud won't show!

I know my Mother would never accept the truth about Dr. Watson and my Daddy would have killed him. I knew she loved me, even if we didn't always agree, I did make her happy.

Mother died peacefully on December 29th, 1991. At her funeral I wrote the eulogy and this is what it said and this is what I believe.

> Tonight I heard your labored breath over the phone as Ann sat by your side waiting for your final hour to come. You haven't really known me for four months now, but on Thanksgiving Day when you said, "I love you J.C." for the last time. It really didn't matter, that you didn't call my name or wonder where I was, because Ann was with you and we were both in your heart.
> You see Mother, you are our Angel, You are our gift from God and over forty years ago, Ann and I were given to you and Daddy to raise.

You did not give us our first breath, or the color of our hair or eyes, but you gave us our life. You protected us against gossip and hurt and pain when you knew and could. You taught us to give and to share and to always be unselfish no matter how little we had. You were always the one there with a custard or soup when someone was in need. You were always there when Ann or I needed anything. Our pain was your pain.

You taught us to love others more than ourselves and forgive those who hurt us because only then could we be free to love again. Most of all you gave us strength and a will to survive all obstacles that come into our lives. You never left us alone. Mother we will miss you, but your love and presence will never leave our side. You are smiling now, you are happy and you are free of pain, at peace. You are with Daddy who you missed so much and love dearly.

Always know that the two baby girls that were entrusted to you so many years ago were so blessed to know you, share your life and love you as their Mother. 12/29/91 JCR

Both of my mothers are gone now and one of my dads for sure, but their strength and ideals live on in Michael and I and I am so proud of who

I am. I was never bad or "tarnished" as I thought my whole life. The people who were mean to me and unkind and Dr. Watson were the "tarnished ones."

Stephen I hope this letter finds you. I'm still a child in so many ways. I can dream and I can see the good in everyone and yet I am a woman wanting a relationship like I never had a chance to have. I want someone to love me who will respect me like my father's respected my mothers. They were real men. Sometimes I still get unsure and frightened but I can deal with it now because I know why, I know the truth.

I don't regret the pain, the scars, or the journey because they made me who I am and I like that. I still laugh and smile and cry and salty tears can flow freely. I'm free of the guilt the pain and I know I had no control over what happened to me. I know my mothers gave me their strength, and my fathers gave me their gentle ways. I know how my

own son, my flesh gave me the will to survive and you Stephen, your blue eyes lit up my life, your lips spoke the words I had always hoped to hear, you made me feel loved whether you meant it or not. You touched my heart, you touched my soul, you shared a part of yourself with me, so I could find my life.
Thank you.

J.C.

...this book is not edited,
...life is not edited,
...no one felt my feelings,
...no one lived my life,
...no one but me.

...to all survivors,
...this is for you
...I understand.

JCR 1993

ABUSE...INCEST...RAPE
They are all the same,
They are done with power to inflict pain.
They are done to children and adults alike,
They are cruel and vicious and never right.

She knew what it felt like,
She knew all the pain,
She lost her life in just such a game.

She was a child afraid,
A child so small,
A child defenseless against it all.

For forty some years her mind hid the truth,
She could not function, she could not blame,
She could never feel love, she could only feel pain.
She could feel only fear for so many years.
A fear that controlled her, a fear set so deep,
She lost the love she tried to seek.

The scars are still there, so deep inside,
Put there by one man with power not pride.
The years are past, the pain is now gone,
The memories fading, her life goes on.

Her eyes are now shining, her smile is so bright,
She has hope for the future in a whole new light.
.........THIS IS MY STORY.........